A TREASURY OF GARDEN VERSE

Published in the United Kingdom Exclusively for

SELECTABOOK
Folly Road
Roundway
Devizes
Wiltshire SN10 2HT

Produced by TAJ BOOKS
27 Ferndown Gardens
Cobham
Surrey
KT11 2BH
United Kingdom

Email : info@tajbooks.com

First published in 1992

Designed by Ian Cameron and Jill Hollis
Typeset in Baskerville by Cameron Books, Moffat
Produced by Cameron Books, PO Box 1, Moffat, Dumfriesshire DG10 9SU, Scotland.
www.cameronbooks.co.uk

ISBN 1-84406-020-9

The artists wishes to thank the following people for allowing her to visit their gardens and gather material for some of the pictures in this book: Mr Murray Holdsworth, Jennie and Dave Kuca, Dick and Peggy Linklater, Mr and Mrs N. Monro, Mrs N.G. Newman, Julia and Arthur Roberts, Mrs Phyllis Stark and Mrs Ethel Waring.

Thanks are due for their permission to reproduce copyright material in this volume: to Faber and Faber to 'Their Lonely Betters' by W.H. Auden from Collected Poems; to Rosemary Seymour for 'Christmas Rose' and 'Gardeners' by Gerald Bullett; to Mrs Nicolette Gray and The Society of Authors on behalf of the Laurence Binyon Estate for an extract from 'The Burning of the Leaves' by Laurence Binyon; to the Estate of Richard Church for 'Allotments' and 'Smelling Chrysanthemums' by Richard Church; to The Literary Trustees of Walter de la Mare and The Society of Authors as their representative for 'Myself' and an extract from 'The Miracle' by Walter de la Mare; to the Literary Executor of Leonard Clark for 'Christmas Rose' and 'Peaches' by Leonard Clark; to Carcanet Press Ltd for 'Pear Tree' by H.D. from Collected Poems 1912-1944; to the Estate of Robert Frost for 'Lodged' from The Poetry of Robert Frost ed. E.C.Lathem and published by Jonathan Cape; to Carcanet Press Ltd for 'Giant Decorative Dahlia' by Molly Holden from Selected Poems; to the Executors of Lilian Bowes Lyon from Collected Poems published by Jonathan Cape; to Carcanet Press for 'For Bonfires I' by Edwin Morgan from Collected Poems; to Kathleen Raine for her 'Sweet-briar Fragrance on the Air'; to Duckworth for 'Wistaria: Tuscan' by Sacheverell Sitwell from Collected Poems; to Granada for 'Kensington Gardens' by Muriel Spark from Going up to Sotheby's and Other Poems; to R.S. Thomas, 53 Gloucester Road, Kew, UK, for his 'The Garden' from The Bread of Truth; to André Deutsch for 'Hoeing' by John Updike from Telephone Poles. Cameron Books has made every effort to obtain permission to reproduce material in copyright and apologises to any copyright holder who has proved impossible to contact.

Wishes

Go, little book, and wish to all
Flowers in the garden, meat in the hall,
A bin of wine, a spice of wit,
A house with lawns enclosing it,
A living river by the door,
A nightingale in the sycamore.

ROBERT LOUIS STEVENSON (1850-1894)

POEMS

To a Snowdrop

Lone flower, hemmed in with snows and white as they
But hardier far, once more I see thee bend
Thy forehead, as if fearful to offend,
Like an unbidden guest. Though day by day,
Storms, sallying from the mountain-tops, waylay
The rising sun, and on the plains descend;
Yet art thou welcome, welcome as a friend
Whose zeal outruns his promise! Blue-eyed May
Shall soon behold this border thickly set
With bright jonquils, their odours lavishing
On the soft west wind and his frolic peers:
Nor will I then thy modest grace forget,
Chaste Snowdrop, venturous harbinger of Spring,
And pensive monitor of fleeting years!

WILLIAM WORDSWORTH (1770-1850)

The Snowdrop

Yes, punctual to the time, thou'rt here again,
As still thou art: though frost or rain may vary,
And icicles blockade the rockbirds' aery,
Or sluggish snow lie heavy on the plain,
Yet thou, sweet child of hoary January,
Art here to harbinger the laggard train
Of vernal flowers, a duteous missionary.
Nor cold can blight, nor fog thy pureness stain.
Beneath the dripping eaves, or on the slope
Of cottage garden, whether mark'd or no,
Thy meek head bends in undistinguish'd row.
Blessings upon thee, gentle bud of hope!
And Nature bless the spot where thou dost grow –
Young life emerging from thy kindred snow!

HARTLEY COLERIDGE (19th century)

from *Kensington Garden*

A flower that first in this sweet garden smil'd
To virgin sacred, and the Snow-drop styl'd . . .

Mid frosts and snows triumphant dares appear,
Mingles the seasons, and leads on the year.

THOMAS TICKELL (1686-1740)

from *The Garden*

Who loves a garden, loves a green-house too.
Unconscious of a less propitious clime,
There blooms exotic beauty, warm and snug,
While the winds whistle and the snows descend.
The spiry myrtle with unwith'ring leaf
Shines there, and flourishes. The golden boast
Of Portugal and western India there,
The ruddier orange, and the paler lime,
Peep through their polish'd foliage at the storm,
And seem to smile at what they need not fear.
Th' amomum there with intermingling flow'rs
And cherries hangs her twigs. Geranium boasts
Her crimson honours, and the spangled beau,
Ficoides, glitters bright the winter long.
All plants, of ev'ry leaf that can endure
The winter's frown, if screen'd from his shrewd bite,
Live there, and prosper . . .

WILLIAM COWPER (1731-1800)

from *June*

When the Spring has dipped her foot,
   Like a bather, in the air,
And the ripples warm the root,
   Till the little flowers dare,
There is promise she will grow
Sweeter than the Springs of old,
Fairer than was ever told.
     Heigh-ho!

HARRISON S. MORRIS (b 1856)

Beauty of Flowers

The flowers are nature's jewels with whose wealth
She decks her summer beauty; primrose sweet,
With blossoms of pure gold; enchanting rose,
That like a virgin queen, salutes the sun,
Dew-diadem'd.

GEORGE CROLY (1780-1860)

A Contemplation upon Flowers

Brave flowers – that I could gallant it like you,
And be as little vain!
You come abroad, and make a harmless show,
And to your beds of earth again.
You are not proud: you know your birth:
For your embroider'd garments are from earth.

You do obey your months and times, but I
Would have it ever Spring:
My fate would know no Winter, never die,
Nor think of such a thing.
O that I could my bed of earth but view
And smile, and look as cheerfully as you!

O teach me to see Death and not to fear,
But rather to take truce!
How often have I seen you at a bier,
And there look fresh and spruce!
You fragrant flowers! then teach me, that my breath
Like yours may sweeten and perfume my death.

HENRY KING (1592-1669)

Sowing

It was a perfect day
For sowing; just
As sweet and dry was the ground
As tobacco-dust.

I tasted deep the hour
Between the far
Owl's chuckling first soft cry
And the first star.

A long stretched hour it was;
Nothing undone
Remained; the early seeds
All safely sown.

And now, hark at the rain,
Windless and light,
Half a kiss, half a tear,
Saying good-night.

EDWARD THOMAS (1878-1917)

Sowing beans

One for the mouse,
One for the crow.
One to rot,
One to grow.

ANONYMOUS

from *A Hundred Good Points of Huswifery*

In Marche and in Aprill, from morning to night:
in sowing and setting, good huswives delight;
To have in a garden, or other like plot:
to trim up their house, and to furnish their pot.

THOMAS TUSSER (c.1524-1580)

from *Upon Appleton House*

See how the flowers, as at parade,
Under their colours stand display'd:
Each regiment in order grows,
That of the tulip, pink, and rose.
But when the vigilant patrol
Of stars walks round about the pole,
Their leaves, that to the stalks are curl'd,
Seem to their staves the ensigns furl'd.

ANDREW MARVELL (1621-1678)

from *Serene is the Morning*

The gay gaudy tulip observe as you walk,
How flaunting the gloss of its vest!
How proud! and how stately it stands on its stalk,
In beauty's diversity drest!
From the rose, the carnation, the pink and the clove,
What odours delightfully spring!
The South wafts a richer perfume to the grove,
As he brushes the leaves with his wing.

WILLIAM WOTY (1731-1791)

Tulips

Let tulips trust not the warm vernal rain,
But dread the frosts and still their blooms restrain;
So when bright Phoebus smiles with kindly care.
The moon not sullied by a lowering air,
Early the beauteous race you'll wondering see,
Ranged in the beds, a numerous progeny:
The tulip with her painted charms display
Through the mild air, and make the garden gay;
The tulip which with gaudy colours stained,
The name of beauty to her race has gained,
For whether she in scarlet does delight,
Chequered and streaked with lines of glittering white,
Or sprinkled o'er with purple charms our sight;
Or widow-like beneath a sable veil,
Her purest lawn does artfully conceal,
Or emulate, the varied agate's veins,
From every flower the beauty's prize obtained.

ABRAHAM COWLEY (1618-1667)

"Auricula"
L. Benton

from *Endymion*

. . . Oft have I brought thee flowers, on their stalks set
Like vestal primroses, but dark velvet
Edges them round, and they have golden pits:
Twas there I got them, from the gaps and slits
In a mossy stone, that sometimes was my seat,
When all above was faint with mid-day heat.

JOHN KEATS (1795-1821)

Auriculas

See how the Bears Eares* in their several dresses,
(That yet no Poet's pen to hight expresses.)
Each head adornèd with such rich attire,
Which Fools and Clowns may slight, whilst skil'd admire.
Their gold, their purples, scarlets, crimson dyes,
Their dark and lighter hair'd diversities.
With all their pretty shades and Ornaments,
Their parti-colour'd coats and pleasing scents.
Gold laid on scarlet, silver on the blew
With sparkling eyes to take the eyes of you.
Mixt colours, many more to please that sense,
Others with rich and great magnificence,
In double Ruffs, with gold and silver laced,
On purple crimson and so neatly placed.
Ransack Flora's wardrobes, none sure can bring
More taking Ornaments t' adorn the spring.

SAMUEL GILBERT (17th century)

*auriculas

Pear Tree

Silver dust,
lifted from the earth,
higher than my arms reach,
you have mounted,
O, silver,
higher than my arms reach,
you front us with great mass;

no flower ever opened
so staunch a white leaf,
no flower ever parted silver
from such rare silver;

O, white pear,
your flower-tufts
thick on the branch
bring summer and ripe fruits
in their purple hearts.

H.D. (1886-1961)

Proportion

In the sky there is a moon and stars,
And in my garden there are yellow moths
Fluttering about a white azalea bush.

AMY LOWELL (1874-1925)

Forget-Me-Not

The blossoms blue to the bank he threw
Ere he sank in the eddying tide;
And 'Lady, I'm gone, thine own knight true,
Forget-me-not', he cried.
The farewell pledge the lady caught,
And hence, as legends say,
The flower is a sign to awaken thought
Of friends who are far away.

ANONYMOUS (19th century)

Forget-Me-Nots

When to the flowers to beautiful
The Father gave a name,
Back came a little blue-eyed one,
All timidly it came.
And standing at its Father's feet,
And gazing in His face,
It said in low and trembling tone,
'Dear God, the name thou gavest me,
Alas! I have forgot.'
Kindly the Father looked Him down,
And said, 'Forget-me-not.'

ANONYMOUS (19th century)

from *When Lilacs Last in the Dooryard Bloom'd*

In the dooryard fronting an old farm-house near the white-wash'd palings,
Stands the lilac-bush tall-growing with heart-shaped leaves of rich green,
With many a pointed blossom rising delicate, with the perfume strong I love,
With every leaf a miracle – and from this bush in the dooryard,
With delicate-color'd blossoms and heart-shaped leaves of rich green,
A sprig with its flower I break.

WALT WHITMAN (1819-1892)

from *The Winter Walk at Noon*

The Lilac, various in array, now white,
Now sanguine, and her beauteous head now set
With purple spikes pyramidal, as if
Studious of ornament, yet unresolved
Which hue she most approved, she chose them all.

WILLIAM COWPER (1731-1800)

from *The Gardener's Daughter*

. . . Lightly he laugh'd, as one that read my thought,
And on he went; but ere an hour had pass'd,
We reach'd a meadow slanting to the north;
Down which a well-worn pathway courted us
To one green wicket in a privet hedge;
This, yielding, gave into a grassy walk
Thro' crowded lilac-ambush trimly pruned;
And one warm gust, full-fed with perfume, blew
Beyond us, as we enter'd in the cool.
The garden stretches soutward. In the midst
A cedar spread his dark-green layers of shade.

ALFRED, LORD TENNYSON (1809-1892)

The Rose

A rose, as fair as ever saw the North,
Grew in a little garden all alone;
A sweeter flower did Nature ne'er put forth,
Nor fairer garden yet was never known:
The maidens danced about it morn and noon,
And learnèd bards of it their ditties made;
The nimble fairies by the pale-faced moon
Water'd the root and kiss'd her pretty shade.
But well-a-day! – the gardener careless grew;
The maids and fairies both were kept away,
And in a drought the caterpillars threw
Themselves upon the bud and every spray.
God shield the stock! If heaven send no supplies,
The fairest blossom of the garden dies.

WILLIAM BROWNE (1588-1643)

Flowers

Yes; there is heaven about you: in your breath
And hues it dwells. The stars of heaven ye shine;
Bright strangers in a land of sin and death,
That talk of God, and point to realms divine . . .

Ye speak of frail humanity: ye tell
How man, like you, shall flourish and shall fail:-
But ah! ye speak of Heavenly Love as well,
And say, the God of flowers is God of all . . .

Sweet flowers, sweet flowers! the rich exuberance
Of Nature's heart in her propitious hours:
When glad emotions in her bosom dance
She vents her happiness in laughing flowers . . .

Childhood and you are playmates; matching well
Your sunny cheeks, and mingling fragrant breath:-
Ye help young Love his faltering tale to tell;
Ye scatter sweetness o'er the bed of Death.

HENRY FRANCIS LYTE (1793-1847)

Wistaria: Tuscan

It has come, it has come again,
This lost blue world
That I have not seen for seven years,
And now there is no other earth beside it.
O what I have missed, these seven eyeless summers,
For this is a blue world shut into itself,
This trellis of wistaria, this blue fire falling;
Its leaves drop flame to every quarter of the winds,
But I lived seven years away and came not to it,
And now the flowers are sevenfold, their honey tongues
Loll like a million bells that quiver and don't ring,
Though the air all trembles and vibrates with them.
Then, as now, their blueness was alive
With quick spangled comedies, quick turncoat rain,
That fell by the trellis and was dyed in that colour;
There was never such a heaping; such a deep piled fullness,

For the flowers lie on the pergola, like snow disastered
From some whirling cataclysm thrown and tumbled.
Let us sit in this cage of fire and think of it!
Why is no poetry so full as this,
But this is mortal with but a breath of life;
Nothing lives outside it, if you keep within,
You have seven days, and a table and a chair;
What else can you wish, you are no prisoner?
Why ever move away from here, there's nothing else?
But keep in this cage of fire and live within it,
Be the salamander in this house of flame;
Look from the windows, see the world on fire.
But now comes the aftermath, the hollow empty bathos,
For this blue flower faded at the bat-winged dusk,
It faded and went out into a lifeless nothing;
Not even did the scent stay in this worse than death.

SACHEVERELL SITWELL (1897-1988)

from *To a Friend, Planting*

Proceed, my Friend, pursue thy healthful toil,
Dispose thy ground, and meliorate thy soil;
Range thy young plants in walks, or clumps, or bow'rs,
Diffuse o'er sunny banks thy fragrant flow'rs;
And, while the new creation round thee springs,
Enjoy uncheck'd the guiltless bliss it brings . . .

JOHN SCOTT (1730-1783)

from *Flora, Ceres and Pomona*

Into your garden you can walk
And with each plant and flower talk;
View all their glories, from each one
Raise some rare meditation.
Recount their natures, tell which are
Vertuous like you, as well as fair.

JOHN REA (d 1681)

Sweet-briar Fragrance on the Air

Sweet-briar fragrance on the air,
Late spring's forget-me-not, and early summer
Saxifrage and poppies, peonies and thyme,
Three young thrushes under the rhubarb leaves,
Broad beans in flower, pansies
Pricked out in boxes, too young for the border.
I have been alone; yet wish earth the better
Because of yet another summer my old eyes have seen
The beauty of this garden, the cattle grazing
Beyond the hawthorn hedge of my quiet acre.

KATHLEEN RAINE (b 1908)

Floral Tribute

*(Stimulated by listening to a laverock or lark,
    while fishing for a chavender or chub)*

The monkey-flower, or mimulus,
    The mimulus, or musk,
That grows beside the Imulus,
    The Imulus or Usk,
Is humble and subfimulus,
    Is modestly subfusc.
Yet, when at evening dimulus,
    When at the falling dusk
I chew the bitter himulus
    Of life, the bitter husk –
Harder than any rimulus
    (A rimulus, or rusk),
Such as might crack a timulus,
    An elephantine tusk –
Then to the stream I bimulus,
    All eagerly I busk,
To gaze on thee, O mimulus,
And from thee draw a stimulus,
    A stimulus, or stusk.

CHARLES JEFFRIES (late 19th/early 20th century

from *The Nymph Complaining for the Death of Her Faun*

I have a garden of my own
But so with roses overgrown
And lilies, that you would it guess
To be a little wilderness.

ANDREW MARVELL (1621-1678)

The Garden

The world's a garden; pleasures are the flowers,
   Of fairest hues, in form and number many:
   The lily, first, pure-whitest flower of any,
Rose sweetest rare, with pinkèd gilliflowers,
The violet, and double marigold,
   And pansy too: but after all mischances,
Death's winter comes and kills with sudden cold
   Rose, lily, violet, marigold, pink, pansies.

JOSHUA SYLVESTER (1563-1618)

from *Silva*

And since the lawless Grass will oft invade
The neighb'ring Walks, repress th' aspiring Blade,
Suffer no Grass or rugged dirt t'impair
Your smoother Paths. But to the Gard'ner's care
These things we leave; they are his Business,
With setting Flowers and planting fruitful Trees:
And with the Master let the Servants join,
With him their willing Hearts and Hands combine,
Some should with Rowlers tame the yielding Ground,
Making it plain where ruder Clods abound.
Some may fit Moisture to your Meadows give,

And so the Plants and Gardens may derive
Refreshing streams; let others sweep away
The fallen Leaves; mend hedges that Decay:
Cut off superfluous Boughs; or with a Spade
Find where the Moles their winding Nests have made;
Then close them up. Another flowers may sow
In Beds prepar'd; on all some Task bestow;
That if the Master happens to come down,
To fly the Smoak and Clamour of the Town,
He in his villa none may idle find,
But secret Joys may please his wearied Mind.

JOHN EVELYN (1620-1706)

My Garden

A garden is a lovesome thing, God wot!
Rose plot,
Fringed pool,
Fern'd grot –
  The veriest school
  Of peace; and yet the fool
Contends that God is not –
Not God! in gardens! when the eve is cool?
Nay, but I have a sign;
'Tis very sure God walks in mine.

T.E. BROWN (1830-1897)

from *The Winter Evening*

What are the casements lin'd with creeping herbs,
The prouder sashes fronted with a range
Of orange, myrtle, or the fragrant weed,
The Frenchman's darling?* are they not all proofs
That man, immur'd in cities, still retains
His inborn inextinguishable thirst
Of rural scenes, compensating his loss
By supplemental shifts, the best he may?
The most unfurnish'd with the means of life,
And they that never pass their brick-wall bounds
To range the fields and treat their lungs with air,
Yet feel the burning instinct: over-head
Suspend their crazy boxes, planted thick,
And water'd duly. There the pitcher stands
A fragment, and the spoutless tea-pot there;
Sad witnesses how close-pent man regrets
The country, with what ardour he contrives
A peep at nature, when he care no more.

WILLIAM COWPER (1731-1800)

*mignonette

Cheddar Pinks

Mid the squander'd colour idling as I lay
Reading the Odyssey in my rock-garden
I espied the cluster'd tufts of Cheddar Pinks
Burgeoning with promise of their scented bloom
All the modish motley of their bloom to-be
Thrust up in narrow buds on the slender stalks
Thronging springing urgent hasting (so I thought)
As if they feared to be too late for summer –
Like schoolgirls overslept waken'd by the bell
Leaping from bed to don their muslin dresses
      On a May morning.

Then felt I like to one indulging in sin
(Whereto Nature is oft a blind accomplice)
Because my aged bones so enjoyed the sun
There as I lay along idling with my thoughts
Reading an old poet while the busy world
Toil'd moil'd fuss'd and scurried worried bought and sold
Plotted stole and quarrel'd fought and God knows what.
I had forgotten Homer dallying with my thoughts
Till I fell to making these little verses
Communing with the flowers in my rock-garden
      On a May morning.

ROBERT BRIDGES (1844-1930)

"Pinks"
L. Kenton

47

Kensington Gardens

Old ladies and tulips, model boats,
Compact babies, mobile mothers,
Distant buses like parakeets,
Lonely men with mackintoshes
Over their arms – where do they go?
Where come from? now that summer's
Paraphernalia and splash is
Out, as if planted a year ago.

MURIEL SPARK (b 1918)

In Kensington Gardens

In Kensington Gardens the poplars
shivered with buds like raindrops, and a chestnut or two
was in young leaf already;
Spring struck a sooty anvil
and green sparks flew upward;
a dog rollicked and tumbled, and the children
of rich parents, lovely and perishable,
flashed in and out of violet and amber glooms.
(Oh their antique laughter
bubbling eternally and fading!)
An old man like a squirrel, and who lacked a larder,
with a sharp stick prodded the leaf mould;
after him came two high-brows playing a wordy ping-pong;
April's confederates,
first-lovers inarticulate with a wooden rapture,
in quiet nooks conceived a garden invisible;
while on a bench Benevolence
ate sandwiches, retailing the crumbs to a multitude.
To such pygmies the sweet day leaning from heaven
let down her shining hair.

LILIAN BOWES LYON (1895-1949)

Red Geranium and Godly Mignonette

Imagine that any mind ever *thought* a red geranium!
As if the redness of a red geranium could be anything but a sensual experience
and as if sensual experience could take place before there were any senses.
We know that even God could not imagine the redness of a red geranium
nor the smell of mignonette
when the geraniums were not, and mignonette neither.
And even when they were, even God would have to have a nose
to smell at the mignonette.
You can't imagine the Holy Ghost sniffing at cherry-pie heliotrope.
Or the Most High, during the coal age, cudgelling his mighty brains
even if he had any brains: straining his mighty brains
to think, among the moss and mud of lizards and mastodons
to think out, in the abstract, when all was twilit green and muddy:
'Now there shall be tum-tiddly-um, and tum-tiddly-um,
hey-presto! scarlet geranium!'
We know it couldn't be done.
But imagine, among the mud and the mastodons
God sighing and yearning with tremendous creative yearning, in that dark green mess
oh, for some other beauty, some other beauty
that blossomed at last, red geranium, and mignonette.

D.H. LAWRENCE (1885-1930)

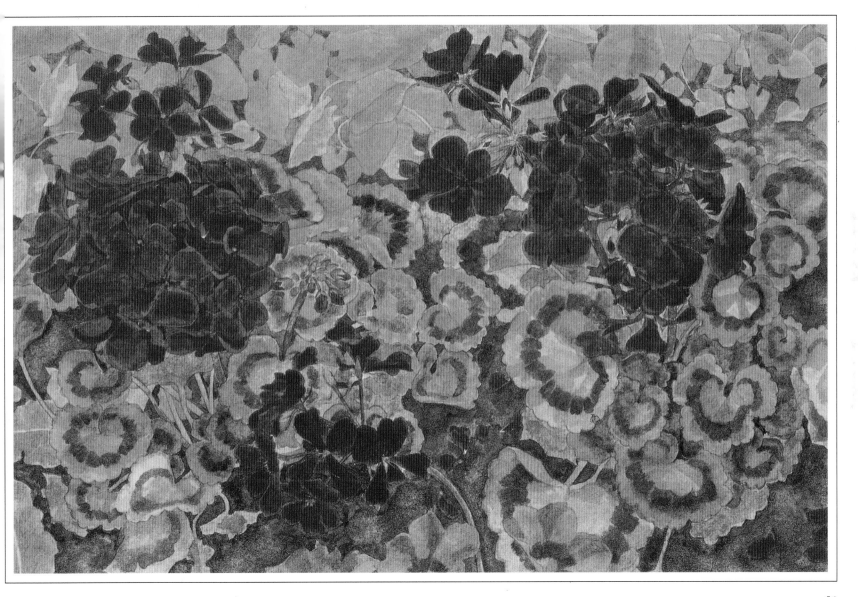

What is a Garden?

What is a garden?
Goodness knows!
You've got a garden,
I suppose!

To one it is a piece of ground
For which some gravel must be found.
To some, those seeds that must be sown,
To some a lawn that must be mown.
To some a ton of Cheddar rocks.
To some it means a window box;
To some, who dare not pick a flower –
A man, at eighteen pence an hour.
To some, it is a silly jest.
About the latest garden pest;
To some, a haven where they find
Forgetfulness and peace of mind . . .

What is a garden?
Large or small,
'Tis just a garden,
After all.

REGINALD ARKELL (1882-1959)

The Garden

It is a gesture against the wild,
The ungovernable sea of grass;
A place to remember love in,
To be lonely for a while;
To forget the voices of children
Calling from a locked room;
To substitute for the care
Of one querulous human
Hundreds of dumb needs.

It is the old kingdom of man.
Answering to their names,
Out of the soil the buds come,
The silent detonations
Of power wielded without sin.

R.S. THOMAS (b 1913)

53

from

'I Stood Tip-toe Upon a Little Hill'

Here are sweet peas, on tip-toe for a flight:
With wings of gentle flush o'er delicate white,
And taper fingers catching at all things,
To bind them all about with tiny rings.

JOHN KEATS (1795-1821)

Lavender

Grey walls that lichen stains,
That take the sun and the rains,
Old, stately, and wise;
Clipt yews, old lawns flag-bordered,
In ancient ways yet ordered;
South walks where the loud bee plies,
Day-long the summer flies; –
Here grows Lavender, here breathes England.

Gay cottage gardens, glad,
Comely, unkempt and mad,
Jumbled, jolly and quaint;
Nooks where some old man dozes;
Currants and beans and roses
Mingling without restraint;
A wicket that long lacks paint; –
Here grows Lavender, here breathes England.

Sprawling for elbow room,
Spearing straight spikes of bloom,
Clean, wayward and tough;
Sweet and tall and slender,
True, enduring and tender,
Buoyant and bold and bluff,
Simplest, sanest of stuff; –
Thus grows Lavender, thence breathes England.

ANONYMOUS (early 20th century)

Lavender

Now summer goes –
Lingers, bestows
One rich last gift of her making –
These, azure-dim,
Odorous, slim,
Lavender blooms for our taking.

So many flowers!
Such shining hours!
Many a bird's sweet 'Come hither.'
Then the rose fades,
Hushed are the glades,
Lavender's sweet, tho' it wither!

Pass them not by,
Silent and shy,
Sober, aloof in their seeming;
Through winter nights
Of June's delights,
Lavender sets us a-dreaming.

AGNES S. FALCONER (19th century)

Their Lonely Betters

As I listened from a beach-chair in the shade
To all the noises that my garden made,
It seemed to me only proper that words
Should be withheld from vegetables and birds.

A robin with no Christian name ran through
The Robin-Anthem which was all it knew,
And rustling flowers for some third party waited
To say which pairs, if any, should get mated.

No one of them was capable of lying,
There was not one which knew that it was dying
Or could have with a rhythm or a rhyme
Assumed responsibility for time.

Let them leave language to their lonely betters
Who count some days and long for certain letters;
We, too, make noises when we laugh or weep,
Words are for those with promises to keep.

W.H. AUDEN (1907-1973)

from *The Month of June*

It is the month of June
The month of leaves and roses,
When pleasant sights salute the eyes
And pleasant scents the noses.

NATHANIEL PARKER WILLIS (1806-1894)

from *The Doors of Eternity*

Thou perceivest the flowers put forth their precious odours,
And none can tell how from so small a centre come such sweets,
Forgetting that within that centre Eternity expands
Its ever-during doors . . .

WILLIAM BLAKE (1757-1827)

from *Swan of Bignor*

The cottage garden, most for use designed,
Is not of beauty destitute. The vine
Mantles the little casement, and the briar
Drops fragrant dew among the July flowers;
And pansies rayed and freaked, with mottled pinks,
Grow among balm, and rosemary, and rue;
There honeysuckles flaunt, and roses blow . . .

CHARLOTTE SMITH (1749-1806)

from *Rural Evening*

Where rustic taste at leisure trimly weaves
The rose and straggling woodbines to the eaves,.
And on the crowded spot that pales enclose
The white and scarlet daisy rears in rows,
And trailing peas in bunches training neat
Perfuming evening with a luscious sweet –
And sunflowers planted for their gilded show,
That scale the window's lattice ere they blow,
And sweet to 'habitants within the sheds,
Peep through the diamond panes their golden heads.

JOHN CLARE (1793-1864)

Roses

Nature responds so beautifully
Roses are only once-wild roses, that were given an extra chance,
So they bloomed out and filled themselves with coloured fulness
Out of sheer desire to be splendid, and more splendid.

D.H. LAWRENCE (1885-1930)

Dew

See how the Orient Dew,
Shed from the Bosom of the Morn
Into the blowing Roses,
Yet careless of its Mansion new;
For the clear Region where t'was born
 Round in its self incloses!
And, in its little Globes Extent,
Frames as it can its native Element –
 How it the purple flow'r does slight,
Scarce touching where it lyes,
But gazing back upon the Skies,
 Shines with a mournful Light,
  Like its own Tear,
Because so long divided from the Sphear.

Restless it roules and unsecure,
Trembling lest it grow impure,
Till the warm Sun pitty its Pain
And to the Skies exhale it back again.
 So the Soul, that Drop, that Ray
Of the clear Fountain of Eternal Day,
Could it within the humane Flow'r be seen
 Remembring still its former height,
Shuns the sweet leaves and blossoms green;
 And, recollecting its own Light,
Does, in its pure and circling thoughts, express
The greater Heaven in a Heaven less . . .

ANDREW MARVELL (1621-1678)

from *Thoughts in a Garden*

How well the skilful gardener drew
Of flowers, and herbs, this dial new,
Where, from above, the milder sun
Does through a fragrant zodiac run,
And, as it works, the industrious bee
Computes its tune as well as we!
How could such sweet and wholesome hours
Be reckoned but with herbs and flowers?

ANDREW MARVELL (1621-1678)

The Butterfly

He the gay garden round about doth fly,
From bed to bed, from one to other border,
And takes survey with curious busy eye
Of every flower and herb there set in order;
Now this, now that, he tasteth tenderly,
Ye none of them he rudely doth disorder,
Ne with his feet their silken leaves deface,
But pastures on the pleasures of each place,

And evermore with most variety
And change of sweetness (for all change is sweet),
He casts his glutton sense to gratify;
Now sucking of the sap of herb most meet,
Or of the dew which yet on them does lie,
Now in the same bathing his tender feet;
And then he percheth on some branch thereby
To weather him, and his moist wings to dry.

EDMUND SPENSER (1552 or 1553-1599)

To a Butterfly

I've watched you now a full half-hour,
Self-poised upon that yellow flower;
And, little Butterfly! indeed
I know not if you sleep or feed
How motionless! – not frozen seas
More motionless! and then
What joy awaits you, when the breeze
Hath found you out among the trees,
And calls you forth again!

This plot of Orchard-ground is ours;
My trees they are, my Sister's flowers;
Here rest your wings when they are weary;
Here lodge as in a sanctuary!
Come often to us, fear no wrong;
Sit near us on the bough!
We'll talk of sunshine and of song,
And summer days, when we were young;
    eet childish days, that were as long

LLIAM WORDSWORTH (1770-1850)

To a Gardener

Friend, in my mountain-side demesne
My plain-beholding, rosy, green
And linnet-haunted garden-ground,
Let still the esculents abound.
Let first the onion flourish there,
Rose among roots, the maiden-fair,
Wine-scented and poetic soul
Of the capacious salad bowl.
Let thyme the mountaineer (to dress
The tinier birds) and wading cress,
The lover of the shallow brook,
From all my plots and borders look.

Nor crisp and ruddy radish, nor
Pease-cods for the child's pinafore
Be lacking: nor of salad clan
The last and least that ever ran
About great nature's garden-beds.
Nor thence be missed the speary heads
Of artichoke; nor thence the bean
That gathered innocent and green
Outsavours the belauded pea.

These tend, I prithee; and for me,
Thy most long-suffering master, bring
In April, when the linnets sing
And the days lengthen more and more
At sundown to the garden door.
And I, being provided thus,
Shall, with superb asparagus,
A book, a taper, and a cup
Of country wine, divinely sup.

R.L. STEVENSON (1850-1894)

A Garden Song

I scorn the doubts and cares that hurt
  The world and all its mockeries,
My only care is now to squirt
  The ferns among my rockeries.

In early youth and later life
  I've seen an up and seen a down,
And now I have a loving wife
  To help me peg verbena down.

Of joys that come to womankind
  The loom of fate doth weave her few,
But here are summer joys entwined
  And bound with golden feverfew,

I've learnt the lessons one and all
  With which the world its sermon stocks,
Now, heedless of a rise or fall,
  I've Brompton and I've German stocks.

In peace and quiet pass our days,
  With nought to vex our craniums,
Our middle beds are all ablaze
  With red and white geraniums.

And like a boy I laugh when she,
  In Varden hat and Varden hose,
Comes slyly up the lawn at me
  To squirt me with the garden hose.

Let him who'd have the peace he needs
  Give all his worldly mumming up,
Then dig a garden, plant the seeds,
  And watch the product coming up.

GEORGE R. SIMS (1847-1922)

On a Fine Crop of Peas being Spoil'd by a Storm

When Morrice views his prostrate Peas,
　By raging Whirlwinds spread,
He wrings his Hands, and in amaze
　He sadly shakes his Head.

Is this the Fruit of my fond Toil,
　My joy, my Pride, my Chear!
Shall one tempestuous Hour thus spoil
　The Labours of a Year!

Oh! what avails, that Day by Day
　I nurs'd the thriving Crop,
And settl'd with my Foot the Clay,
　And rear'd the social Prop!

Ambition's Pride had spur'd me on
　All Gard'ners to excel;
I often call'd them one by one,
　And boastingly would tell,

How I prepar'd the furrow'd Ground,
　And how the Grain did sow,
Then challeng'd all the Country round
　For such an early Blow.

How did their Bloom my Wishes raise!
　What Hopes did they afford,
To earn my honour'd Master's Praise,
　And crown his chearful Board!

Poor Morrice, wrapt in sad Surprise,
　Demands in sober Mood,
Should Storms molest a Man so wise,
　A Man so just and good?

Ah! Morrice, cease thy fruitless Moan,
Nor at Misfortunes spurn,
Misfortune's not thy Lot alone;
　Each Neighbour has his Turn.

Thy prostrate Peas, which low recline
　Beneath the Frowns of Fate,
May teach much wiser Heads than thine
　Their own uncertain State.

The sprightly Youth in Beauty's Prime,
　The lovely Nymph so gay,
Oft Victims fall to early Time,
　And in their Bloom decay.

In vain th'indulgent Father's Care,
　In vain wise Precepts form:
They droop, like Peas, in tainted Air,
　Or perish in a Storm.

HENRY JONES (1721-1770)

The Garden

The ordered curly and plain cabbages
Are all set out like school-children in rows;
In six short weeks shall these no longer please,
For with that ink-proud lady the rose, pleasure goes.

I cannot think what moved the poet men
So to write panegyrics of that foolish
Simpleton – while wild rose as fresh again
Lives, and the drowsed cabbages keep soil coolish.

IVOR GURNEY (1890-1937)

from *Songs and Chorus of the Flowers*

We are slumberous poppies,
   Lords of Lethe downs,
Some awake, and some asleep,
   Sleeping in our crowns.
What perchance our dreams may know,
Let our serious beauty show.

Central depth of purple,
   Leaves more bright than rose,
Who shall tell what brightest thought
   Out of darkest grows?
Who, through what funereal pain,
Souls to love and peace attain?

LEIGH HUNT (1784-1859)

The Poppies in the Garden

The poppies in the garden, they all wear frocks of silk,
Some are purple, some are pink, and others white as milk,
Light, light, for dancing in, for dancing when the breeze
Plays a little two-step for the blossoms and the bees.
Fine, fine, for dancing in, all frilly at the hem,
Oh, when I watch the poppies dance I long to dance like them!

The poppies in the garden have let their silk frocks fall
All about the border paths, but where are they at all?
Here a frill and there a flounce – a rag of silky red,
But not a poppy-girl is left – I think they've gone to bed.
Gone to bed and gone to sleep; and weary they must be,
For each has left her box of dreams upon the stem for me.

FFRIDA WOLFE (late 19th/early 20th century)

from *Thyrsis*

Soon will the high Midsummer pomps come on,
   Soon will the musk carnation break and swell,
Soon shall we have gold-dusted snap-dragon,
   Sweet William with its homely cottage smell,
   And stocks in fragrant blow;
Roses that down the alleys shine afar,
   And open, jasmine-muffled lattices,
   And groups under the dreaming garden-trees,
And the full moon and the white evening-star.

MATTHEW ARNOLD (1822-1888)

Old-fashioned Flowers

   Dear old-fashioned flowers!
Which filled with ecstasy my childhood's hours,
Sweetwilliams in all quaint varieties,
Pinks and Carnations; surely such as these,
Ere all the beds with foreign blooms were gay,
Our great grand-parents on their wedding day
Exchanged with bows and slow civilities.

AUGUSTUS TAYLOR (late 19th/early 20th century)

from *The Cross Roads or Haymaker's Story*

And where the marjoram once, and sage and rue,
And balm and mint, with curled-leaf parsley grew,
And double marigolds, and silver thyme,
And pumpkins 'neath the window used to climb,
And where I often, when a child for hours
Tried through the pales to get the tempting flowers;
As lady's laces everlasting peas
True loves lies bleeding, with the hearts at ease;
And golden rods, and tansy running high,
That o'er the pale tops smiled on passers-by;
Flowers in my time that every one would praise,
Though thrown like weeds from gardens now-a-days.

JOHN CLARE (1793-1864)

from *Daphnis to Ganymede*

. . . I have a garden plot,
   Wherein there wants nor hearbs, nor roots, nor flowers:
Flowers to smell, roots to eate, hearbs for the pot,
And dainty shelters when the welkin lowers:
   Sweet-smelling beds of lillies, and of roses,
   Which rosemary banks and lavender incloses.

There growes the gillifloure, the mynt, the dayzie
Both red and white, the blue-veynd violet;
The purple hyacinth, the spyke to please thee,
The scarlet dyde carnation bleeding yet:
   The sage, the savery, and sweet margerum,
   Isop, tyme, and eye-bright, good for the blinde and dumbe.

The pinke, the primrose, cowslip and daffadilly,
The hare-bell blue, the crimson cullumbine,
Sage, lettis, parsley, and the milke-white lilly,
The rose and speckled flowre cald sops-in-wine,
   Fine pretie king-cups, and the yellow bootes,
   That growes by rivers and by shallow brookes.

RICHARD BARNFIELD (1574-1627)

Hoeing

I sometimes fear the younger generation will be deprived
   of the pleasures of hoeing;
    there is no knowing
how many souls have been formed by this simple exercise.

The dry earth like a great scab breaks, revealing
   moist-dark loam –
    the pea-root's home,
a fertile wound perpetually healing.

How neatly the green weeds go under!
   The blade chops the earth new.
   Ignorant the wise boy who
has never performed this simple, stupid, and useful wonder.

JOHN UPDIKE (b 1932)

The Poor Man's Garden

Yes! in the poor man's garden grow,
Far more than herbs and flowers,
Kind thoughts, contentment, peace of mind,
And joy for weary hours.

MARY HOWITT (1799-1888)

Time

'Established' is a good word, much used
                           in garden books,
'The plant, when established' . . .
Oh, become established, quickly, quickly, garden!
For I am fugitive, I am very fugitive –

Those that come after me will gather these roses,
And watch, as I do now, the white wistaria
Burst, in the sunshine, from its pale green sheath.

Planned. Planted. Established. Then neglected,
Till at last the loiterer by the gate will wonder
At the old, old cottage, the old wooden cottage,
And say, 'One might build here, the view is glorious;
This must have been a pretty garden once.'

MARY URSULA BETHELL (1874-1945)

from *Of Plants*

The flamy *Pansie* ushers *Summer* in,
His friendly March with *Summer* does begin;
Autumn's Companion too (so *Prosperpine*
Hides half the Year, and half the Year is seen.)
The *Violet* is less beautiful than thee,
That of one Colour boasts, and thou of three.
Gold, Silver, Purple, are thy Ornament,
Thy Rivals thou mightest scorn, hadst thou but Scent.

ABRAHAM COWLEY (1618-1667)

A Flower-Piece by Fantin

Heart's ease or pansy, pleasure or thought,
Which would the picture give us of these?
Surely the heart that conceived it sought
        Heart's ease.

Surely by glad and divine degrees
The heart impelling the hand that wrought
Wrought comfort here for a soul's disease.

Deep flowers, with lustre and darkness fraught,
From glass that gleams as the chill still seas
Lean and lend for a heart distraught
        Heart's ease.

ALGERNON CHARLES SWINBURNE (1837-1909)

Heart's-Ease

The queenly rose, the bright laburnum,
   The pinks – a fragrant crowd,
Forget-me-not and gay nasturtium,
   Wisteria – a cloud;
All have their charms, but none of these
Is dearer than the trim heart's-ease.

Beside the borders brightly smiling
   With modest dewy eyes,
In sunshine and in shade beguiling
   Each swift hour as it flies!
The flow'rs of joy and love may please,
But what are they without heart's-ease?

NORA C. USHER (19th century)

from *Of Plants*

The *Holihock* disdains the common size
Of Herbs, and like a Tree do's proudly rise;
Proud she appears, but try her and you'll find
No Plant more mild, or friendly to Mankind.
She gently all Obstructions do's unbind.

ABRAHAM COWLEY (1618-1667)

A Hollyhock

Seraglio of the Sultan Bee!
I listen at the waxen door,
And hear the zithern's melody
And sound of dancing on the floor.

FRANK DEMPSTER SHERMAN (1860-1916)

from *The Miracle*

Who bids the hollyhock uplift
    Her rod of fast-sealed buds on high;
Fling wide her petals – silent, swift,
        Lovely to the sky?

WALTER DE LA MARE (1873-1956)

from *The Wish*

Well then; I now do plainly see
This busie world and I shall ne're agree;
The very *Honey* of all earthly joy
   Does of all meats the soonest *cloy*;
   And they (methinks) deserve my pity
Who for it can endure the stings,
The *Crowd* and *Buz*, and *Murmurings*
   Of this great *Hive*, the *City*.

   Ah, yet, e're I descend to th' Grave
May I a *small House*, and *large Garden* have!
And a *few Friends*, and many Books, both true,
   Both wise, and both delightful too!
   And since *Love* ne're will from me flee,
A *Mistress* moderately fair,
And good as *Guardian-Angels* are,
   Only belov'd, and loving me!

ABRAHAM COWLEY (1618-1667)

Love in a Mist

Light love in a mist, by the midsummer moon misguided,
Scarce seen in the twilight garden if gloom insist,
Seems vainly to seek for a star whose gleam has derided
    Light love in a mist.

All day in the sun, when the breezes do all they list,
His soft blue raiment of cloudlike blossom abided
Unrent and unwithered of winds and of rays that kissed.

Blithe-hearted or sad, as the cloud or the sun subsided,
Love smiled in the flower with a meaning whereof none wist,
Save two that beheld, as a gleam that before them glided,
    Light love in a mist.

ALGERNON CHARLES SWINBURNE (1837-1909)

A Garden Song

Here in this sequester'd close
Bloom the hyacinth and rose,
Here beside the modest stock
Flaunts the flaring hollyhock;
Here, without a pang, one sees
Ranks, conditions, and degrees.

All the seasons run their race
In this quiet resting-place;
Peach and apricot and fig
Here will ripen and grow big;
Here is store and overplus, –
More had not Alcinoüs!

Here, in alleys cool and green,
Far ahead the thrush is seen;
Here along the southern wall
Keeps the bee his festival;
All is quiet else – afar
Sounds of toil and turmoil are.

Here be shadows large and long
Here be spaces meet for song;
Grant, a garden-god, that I,
Now that none profane is nigh, –
Now that mood and movement please, –
Find the fair Pierides!

HENRY AUSTIN DOBSON (1840-1924)

Gardeners

Gardeners are good. Such vices as they have
Are like the warts and bosses in the wood
Of an old oak. They're patient, stubborn folk,
As needs must be whose busyness it is
To tutor wildness, making war on weeds.
With slow sagacious words and knowing glance
They scan the sky, do all that mortals may
To learn civility to pesty birds
Come after new green peas, cosset and prune
Roses, wash with lime the orchard trees,
Make sun-parlours for seedlings.
                                    Patient, stubborn.
Add cunning next, unless you'd put it first;
For while to dig and delve is all their text
There's cunning in their fingers to persuade
Beauty to bloom and riot to run right,
Mattock and spade, trowel and rake and hoe
Being not tools to learn by learning rules
But extra limbs these husbands of the earth
Had from their birth. Of malice they've no more
Than snaring slugs and wireworms will appease,
Or may with ease be drowned in mugs of mild.
Wherefore I say again, whether or no
It is their occupation makes them so,
Gardeners are good, in grain.

GERALD BULLETT (1893-1958)

Allotments

Lifting through the broken clouds there shot
A searching beam of golden sunset-shine.
It swept the town allotments, plot by plot,
And all the digging clerks became divine –
Stood up like heroes with their spades of brass,
Turning the ore that made the realms of Spain!
So shone they for a moment. Then, alas!
The cloud-rift closed; and they were clerks again.

RICHARD CHURCH (1893-1972)

The Glory of the Garden

Our England is a garden that is full of stately views,
Of borders beds and shrubberies, and lawns and avenues,
With statues on the terraces and peacocks strutting by;
But the glory of the garden lies in more than meets the eye.

For where the old thick laurels grow, along the thin red wall
You find the tool and potting-sheds which are the heart of all;
The cold frames and the hothouses, the dungpits and the tanks,
The rollers, carts and drainpipes, with the barrows and the
    planks.

And there you'll see the gardeners, the men and 'prentice boys
Told off to do as they are bid, and do it without noise;
For except when seeds are planted and we shout to scare the
    birds.
The Glory of the Garden it abideth not in words.

And some can pot begonias, and some can bud a rose,
And some are hardly fit to trust with anything that grows;
But they can roll and trim the lawns and sift the sand and loam,
For the Glory of the Garden occupieth all who come.

Our England is a garden, and such gardens are not made
By singing: 'Oh, how beautiful', and sitting in the shade,
While better men than we go out and start their working lives
At grubbing weeds from gravel paths with broken dinner knives.

There's not a pair of legs so thin, there's not a head so thick,
There's not a hand so weak and white, nor yet a heart so sick,
But it can find some needful work that's crying to be done,
For the Glory of the Garden glorifieth everyone.

Then seek your job with thankfulness and work till further
    orders,
If it's only netting strawberries or killing slugs on borders;
And when your back stops aching and your hands begin to
    harden,
You will find yourself a partner in the Glory of the Garden.

Oh, Adam was a gardener, and God who made him sees
That half a proper gardener's work is done upon his knees,
So when your work is finished, you can wash your hands and
    pray
For the Glory of the Garden, that it may not pass away!
And the Glory of the Garden it shall never pass away!

RUDYARD KIPLING (1865-1936)

The Marigold

Mark how the bashful morn in vain
　　Courts the amorous Marigold,
With sighing blasts and weeping rain;
　　Yet she refuses to unfold.
But when the Planet of the Day
Approacheth with his powerful ray,
　　Then she spreads, then she receives
　　His warmer beams into her virgin leaves.

THOMAS CAREW (c.1595-c.1639)

from 'I Stood Tip-toe Upon a Little Hill'

Open afresh your round of starry folds,
Ye ardent marigolds!
Dry up the moisture of your golden lids,
For great Apollo bids
That in these days your praises should be sung
On many harps, which he has lately strung.

JOHN KEATS (1795-1821)

To Marygolds

Give way, and be ye ravisht by the Sun,
(And hang the head when as the Act is done)
Spread as He spreads; wax lesse as He do's wane;
And as He struts, close up to Maids again.

ROBERT HERRICK (1591-1674)

from To Penshurst

Then hath thy orchard fruit, thy garden flowers,
    Fresh as the ayre, and new as are the houres.
The early cherry, with the later plum,
    Fig, grape, and quince, each in his time doth come;
The blushing apricot, and woolly peach
    Hang on thy walls, that every child may reach.
And though thy walls be of the countrey stone,
    They are rear'd with no mans ruine, no mans grone,
There's none, that dwell about them, wish them downe;
    But all come in, the farmer, and the clowne:
And no one empty-handed, to salute
    Thy lord, and lady, though they have no sute.

BEN JONSON (1572-1637)

from *August*

About the edges of the yellow corn,
And o'er the gardens, grown somewhat out-worn
The bees went hurrying to fill up their store;
The apple-boughs bent over more and more;
With peach and apricot the garden wall,
Was odorous, and the pears begin to fall
From off the high tree with each freshening breeze.

WILLIAM MORRIS (1834-1896)

Peaches

The house, Regency,
the walled garden hushed in the sun,
tidy and formal as a page of Bach;
a few old peach trees
espaliered on the warm brick,
a line of little crucifixions facing south,
with victoria plums, comice pears.
Each velvet globe plucked from the branch,
precious as jewels, held to the cheek,
downy, softer than fawn's coat,
young girl's bloom, gently placed
in chip basket, still holding the day's heat.
And then the teeth sinking into firm flesh
deep to the furrowed stone,
honey juice dribbling down.
Think then of California, Virginia,
prodigal orchards ripening there,
peaches common as crab apples
littering the countryside all the days of fall,
feeding gross pigs, sweetening their hams,
trucks spilling over, or casually tossed
to rot in wasp-hunted heaps,
the air thick with smell of decay.
But here are rare and serenely beautiful,
the household glad and grateful at the sight
of twenty peaches on a September morning,
a child proud to be chosen for the first bite,
the garden sighing in the sun.

LEONARD CLARK (1905-1981)

Giant Decorative Dahlia

It is easy enough to love flowers but these
had never appealed to me before, so
out of proportion above my garden's
other coloured heads and steady stems.

This spring though, in warm soil, I set
an unnamed tuber, offered cheap, and,
when August came and still no sign,
assumed the slugs had eaten it.

              Suddenly it showed;
began to grow, became a small tree.
It was a race between the dingy bud
and the elements. It has beaten
the frost, rears now three feet above
the muddled autumn bed, barbaric petals
pink quilled with tangerine, turning
its great innocent face towards me
triumphantly through the damp afternoon.

I could not deny it love if I tried.

MOLLY HOLDEN (1927-1981)

The Sunflower

Ah, Sun-flower; weary of time,
    Who countest the steps of the Sun;
Seeking after that sweet golden clime,
    Where the traveller's journey is done;
Where the youth pined away with desire,
    And the pale virgin, shrouded in snow
Arise from their graves, and aspire
    Where my Sun-flower wishes to go.

WILLIAM BLAKE (1757-1827)

from *The Mill Garden*

Stately stand the sunflowers, glowing down the garden-side,
Ranged in royal rank arow along the warm grey wall,
Whence their deep disks burn at rich midnoon afire with pride,
Even as though their beams indeed were sunbeams, and the tall
Sceptral stems bore stars whose reign endures, not flowers that fall.

ALGERNON CHARLES SWINBURNE (1837-1909)

To Chrysanthemums

Late comers! Ye, when autumn's wealth is past;
    When pale October strips the yellowing leaves;
    When on our garden lawns and dripping eaves
    The rain-soaked foliage of the elm is cast.
When 'neath grey skies the wild Atlantic blast
    Searches the flowerbed for each bloom that cleaves
    To blackening tendrils; when November weaves
    Fretwork of frost, and winter frowns at last;
Ye in the year's decay and death of hope
    Dawn with your hues auroral, hues of rose,
    Saffron and ivory, amber, amethyst;
More delicate, more dear, more true than those
    Gay blossoms which the July sunbeams kissed,
    Purer of scent than honey heliotrope.

JOHN ADDINGTON SYMONDS (1840-1893)

Smelling Chrysanthemums

This is an ancient scent. I recognise it
For what it isn't, something I recall
From childhood, a perfume heavy with the fall
Of early years. Though common sense denies it,
I still believe that waftage from the past
To be some privilege, sent to me below
As though I were a prince incognito
Waiting a sign, to claim my realm at last.

If this was vanity, I think I share it
With all young living creatures, who in youth
Have twitched their noses in the quest for truth
And found a joy too great for them to bear it
A pardonable vice, to recall in flowers
A royalty that once we knew was ours.

RICHARD CHURCH (1893-1972)

Michaelmas Daisies

'Tis more than mid-October, yet along the narrow garden
The daisies loved of Michaelmas keep sturdily in flower;
For though the evenings sharply fall, they find a way to harden
The crop of comely blossoming that makes for me a bower.

The honey-hunters, diligent, are searching them for sweetness;
A pair of handsome bluetits flash their colours on a stem
(Exponents of the art of standing upside-down with neatness)
While two entranced Red Admirals gaze stonily at them.

The rose has faded bedward, there to dream of scarlet duty
When June is kissing England at the flowertide of the year;
The gladiolus in his bulb considers plans for beauty
To flame along the border when his miracle is clear.

Yet autumn wears an apron, and the apron's sweet with lendings
Of colours matched with comeliness of blossom and of leaf;
And daisies dear to Michaelmas, with dances and with bendings,
Forbid my heart to weary for the Summer's beauteous sheaf.

The garden's fate not narrowly resembles my condition,
With Spring and Summer gone afield delighting other places;
Where towered the hollyhock of Hope, the larkspur of
  Ambition,
Unvaunting blossoms, pale but sweet, have learned to show
  their faces.

Though Time has thinned my lavender and plucked my reddest
  roses,
(He's welcome to the buttonhole he gathered in my ground!)
His picking of a loveliness fresh loveliness uncloses –
Some overshadowed pansy that my heart had never found.

What though he made a nosegay of the fairest and the tallest?
My loving fingers still can tend some simples in the dusk.
'Tis easy to be patient. I will think the best is smallest,
And water here good-humouredly my little pot of musk.

Old Time has made a nosegay. He is welcome to his plucking
Of tiger-lilies, lad's love, and the tall cathedral spires
Of lupins, and snapdragons where the bee is fond of sucking.
And all the flowery likenesses of Youth and Youth's desires.

Old Time has got my nosegay; but the gloaming finds me cheery,
Because the gloaming is itself a flower of lovely hue!
The more I look at what remains, the less of world seems dreary,
For quiet breathes at Michaelmas, and well-worn friends are
  true.

Ah! quiet breathes at Michaelmas, and Love, his bosom sober,
Has got the perfect song by heart and hums it all the day,
To thrill me without feverings and teach how mid-October
Gives angels for the blossoms that old Time has borne away.

NORMAN GALE (1862-1942)

Of Composts

Of composts shall the Muse descend to sing,
Nor soil her heavenly plumes? The sacred Muse
Naught sordid deems, but what is base; naught fair
Unless true Virtue stamp it with her seal.
Then, planter, wouldst thou double thy estate
Never, ah, never, be asham'd to tread
Thy dung-heaps.

JAMES GRAINGER (1721-1766)

from *September*

My song is half a sigh
Because my green leaves die;
Sweet are my fruits, but all my leaves are dying;
And well may Autumn sigh,
And well may I
Who watch the sere leaves flying.

My leaves that fade and fall,
I note you one and all;
I call you, and the Autumn wind is calling,
Lamenting for your fall,
And for the path
You spread on earth in falling.

CHRISTINA ROSSETTI (1830-1894)

from *The Lotos-Eaters*

Lo! sweeten'd with the summer light,
The full juiced apple, waxing over-mellow,
Drops in a silent autumn night.
All its allotted length of days,
The flower ripens in its place,
Ripens and fades, and falls, and hath no toil,
Fast rooted in the fruitful soil.

ALFRED, LORD TENNYSON (1809-1892)

Autumn

"The Spirits of the Air live on the smells
Of fruit; and Joy, with pinions light, roves round
The gardens, or sits singing in the trees,"
Thus sang the jolly Autumn as he sat;
Then rose, girded himself, and o'er the bleak
Hills fled from our sight: but left his golden load.

WILLIAM BLAKE (1757-1827)

Lodged

The rain to the wind said
'You push and I'll pelt!'
They so struck the garden bed
That the flowers actually knelt –
And lay lodged – though not dead.
I know how the flowers felt.

ROBERT FROST (1874-1963)

from *The Loves of the Plants*

When o'er the cultured lawns and dreary wastes
Retiring Autumn flings her howling blasts,
Bends in tumultuous waves the struggling woods,
And showers their leafy honours on the floods,
In withering heaps collects the flowery spoil,
And each chill insect sinks beneath the soil;
Quick flies fair TULIPA the loud alarms,
And folds her infant closer in her arms;
In some lone cave, secure pavilion, lies,
And waits the courtship of serener skies.–

So to his mossy couch the Dormouse springs,
And sleep protects him with his eider wings.–
Bright out of earth, amid the driving storm,
Ascend, fair COLCHICA! thy roseate form
Warms the cold bosom of the hoary year,
And lights with Beauty's blaze the dusky sphere.

ERASMUS DARWIN (1731-1802)

For Bonfires
I

The leaves are gathered, the trees are dying
for a time.
A seagull cries through white smoke in the garden fires
that fill the heavy air.
All day heavy air
is burning, a moody dog
Sniffs and circles the swish of the rake.
In streaks of ash, the gardener drifting
ghostly, beats his hands, a cloud
of breath to the red sun.

EDWIN MORGAN (b 1920)

from *The Burning of the Leaves*

Now is the time for the burning of the leaves.
They go to the fire; the nostril pricks with smoke
Wandering slowly into a weeping mist.
Brittle and blotched, ragged and rotten sheaves!
A flame seizes the smouldering ruin and bites
On stubborn stalks that crackle as they resist.

The last hollyhock's fallen tower is dust;
All the spices of June are a bitter reek,
All the extravagant riches spent and mean.
All burns! The reddest rose is a ghost;
Sparks whirl up, to expire in the mist: the wild
Fingers of fire are making corruption clean.

Now is the time for stripping the spirit bare,
Time for the burning of days ended and done,
Idle solace of things that have gone before:
Rootless hopes and fruitless desire are there;
Let them go to the fire, with never a look behind
The world that was ours is a world that is ours no more.

They will come again, the leaf and the flower to arise
From squalor of rottenness into the old splendour,
And magical scents to a wondering memory bring;
The same glory, to shine upon different eyes.
Earth cares for her own ruins, naught for ours.
Nothing is certain, only the certain spring.

LAURENCE BINYON (1869-1943)

Digging

Today I think
Only with scents – scents dead leaves yield,
And bracken, and wild carrot's seed,
And the square mustard field;

Odours that rise
When the spade wounds the root of tree,
Rose, currant, raspberry, or goutweed,
Rhubarb or celery;

The smoke's smell, too,
Flowing from where a bonfire burns
The dead, the waste, the dangerous,
And all to sweetness turns.

It is enough
To smell, to crumble the dark earth,
While the robin sings over again
Sad songs of Autumn mirth.

EDWARD THOMAS (1878-1917)

from *Winter*

A white flake here and there – a snow lily
    Of last night's frost – our naked flower-beds hold;
    And for a rose-flower on the darkening mould
The hungry redbreast gleams. No bloom, no bee.

DANTE GABRIEL ROSSETTI (1828-1882)

Myself

There is a garden, grey
   With mists of autumntide;
Under the giant boughs,
   Stretched green on every side,

Along the lonely paths,
   A little child like me,
With face, with hands, like mine,
   Plays ever silently;

On, on, quite silently,
   When I am there alone,
Turns not his head; lifts not his eyes;
   Heeds not as he plays on.

After the birds are flown
   From singing in the trees,
When all is grey, all silent,
   Voices, and winds, and bees;

And I am there alone:
   Forlornly, silently,
Plays in the evening garden
   Myself with me.

WALTER DE LA MARE (1873-1956)

Christmas Rose

Wing'd blossom of white thought, yellow-centred
Star of fertility sprung from December soil,
Six perfect petal-rays of frozen light:

See, under the stark oak, in her nest
Of long, serrated, green, environing leaves,
Where like a bird she listens and looks out,

See now, at twilight, how her pale presence,
Even between sundown and dawning star,
Fills the dusk with quickness, quiet as prayer.

GERALD BULLETT (1893-1958)

Christmas Rose

Midwinter, and the dead earth
Suddenly parts to give birth
To thick clusters of stiff flowers
Whiter than scattered pear tree showers,
Marble monuments or morning milk,
Smoother than pebbles or old silk,
I touch each blossom, where they lie
With polished leaves and golden eye,
The hellebore of the January snows,
The plant I call the Christmas rose.

LEONARD CLARK (1905-1981)

Winter Revery

Now let the garden sleep.
Bank the red coals of your impatience
Under the ash of prunings and raked leaves
And swing your eager glance
By the late-rising, early-setting sun's
Short and remoter arc. This is no time to sweep
The quiet, self-sufficient dark with flame.
Earth has forgotten fire, to light indifferent grown.
Night and the North alone attend her now.
Colder than ocean, cold as stone her blood,
Her pulses slow in long, libational rhythms.
Therefore if you would haunt the leafless paths,
Ally, not alien, go in winter's way.
Not one superfluous candle in your eyes,
Nor heat of haste searing the ground with footprints.
Rather in shoes heavy with gathered snow
Or padded with the cling of sodden leaves,
Your breath a cloud of chilly vapor,
Drift through the barren quiet like a sleepy mist
That coldly mingles with an austere dream.

SARA BARD FIELD (1882-?)

from *Faery Song*

Shed no tear! O shed no tear!
The flowers will bloom another year.
Weep no more! O weep no more!
Young buds sleep in the root's white core.

JOHN KEATS (1795-1821)